Creative Cooking

Lizzie McCall

DEDICATION

To those I feed.

CONTENTS

FOREWORD

My philosophy on food is that you should enjoy what you eat and eat what you enjoy. Try new flavours and textures, don't dismiss anything - imagine if you'd refused chocolate the first time you'd been offered it as a baby; wow! Variety is vital to staying healthy, in my opinion. I don't always practice what I preach and go through greedy phases when work is tough, but on the whole, eating a varied diet does not make me put on weight, in fact I lose it steadily. Oh, and read recipes from whatever source you find stimulating but, apart from baking and pastry type dishes, or things which need to set, alter the ingredients as you see fit. No one should tell you what you will enjoy, they can only suggest.

I'm determined my children will have a healthy attitude to food - that they will enjoy vegetables and all things healthy, but that they will also be happy to try new things. They will not see certain items as food 'sins.' Who even invented that word? No food should be a sin, but you just shouldn't eat a cream based meal, a box of chocolates and a fry up all in the same week (or maybe even month, but that's for you to decide!).

Nothing delights me more than seeing my daughters taste all the cheeses, and I mean all the cheeses I buy. Wow. And they fight for gherkins or balsamic pickled onions if they happen to be available. Spicy chorizo and all kinds of saucisson pass their lips with joy if ever we have them, usually for a Saturday night tea, which should always be a bit more special and has extra funding allocated.

So I have decided, as a full time working mum, who works long days and late into the evenings, that I will share my ideas about food. If even one person makes a healthier, cheaper or simply different meal that they've never had before I will be over the moon. I cook many meals in bulk and that is time consuming but during the week, rarely does a meal take longer to make than the time it takes to cook pasta or rice - unless it spends time in the oven, of course, but that doesn't count, as I can be working in the meantime!

Friday? It's pizza night, homemade without fail. Make a base, add tomato puree mixed with minced garlic, top with grated mozzarella and then bob's your uncle. When I was pregnant I lost the energy to make fresh pizza, so every month I made four times the amount, split it, rolled each one, wrapped it in tin foil and froze it. On returning from work, I grabbed a base from the freezer, put it on a pizza tray and topped it. It then went straight into the oven; a doddle.

Saturdays are special and if I can experiment I will. I don't mind spending the whole day cooking for a dinner party, I find it relaxes me. But then I will also happily serve Ina Garten's Steakhouse Steak and homemade chips. It is Saturday, after all!

RULES, MEASUREMENTS & GENERAL HINTS

- Pastry needs precise measurements, so I rarely make it – buy pre-made pastry if you want to use it. Other than that, my theory with cooking is: add whatever you think tastes good.
- I have written quantities rather than measurements where possible, when buying, buy the nearest size pack if necessary.
- Buy olive oil for cooking and use only extra virgin olive oil for salad dressings. Extra virgin olive oil is more expensive but loses the flavour you pay for if cooked. Use vegetable oil for deep frying as it is cheaper and works.
- You will get more juice from a lemon when it is room temperature.
- When you wash herbs be very gentle and use a salad spinner to dry if you can. Chop anything but salad leaves with scissors – tear salad.
- Have a tub of butter in the fridge – it lasts for ages and won't hurt if you don't use it all of the time – a bit of what you fancy ;-)
- Ditto Parmesan – buy a triangle and whilst expensive, it will save in a sealed container or bag for months and just grate what you want – don't ever buy pre-grated in a tub!
- Ditto jars of spices – they will last, (though fridge not needed....)
- Tip: If a meal is over-salted, add sugar or ketchup if tomato-based – usually helps
- Buy a bay leaf plant, thyme, rosemary and mint – pot them well and they should grow well
- At the end of the week, any tomatoes in the fridge can be tossed in a little olive oil and roasted at 180 for an hour or two. They'll keep in an airtight container in the fridge and are great for adding to meals and lunches.
- For lunches, use new potatoes (tins will do!), quinoa, bulgar wheat, couscous, rice (brown or white) and add chopped onion, tomato, cucumber, capers, gherkins – whatever you like – and then add a bit of a dressing. Easy and healthy.

DRESSINGS

Balsamic Vinegar Dressing

Extra virgin olive oil
Balsamic vinegar
Salt
Pepper

- In a jar, mix about 2 parts oil to vinegar – shake to mix if possible
- Taste and adjust to taste
- Season

Lemon and Mustard Dressing

Extra virgin olive oil
Lemon Juice
Salt
Pepper
1 teaspoon mustard or so
Garlic, crushed

- In a jar, mix about 2 parts juice to vinegar
- Add mustard – shake to mix if possible, it will thicken
- Add garlic (if you want to)
- Taste and adjust oil / lemon to taste
- Season

Vinagrette

Extra virgin olive oil
Wine vinegar (or whatever works)
Garlic
Salt
Pepper

- In a jar, mix about 2 parts oil to vinegar – shake to mix if possible

- Add garlic
- Taste and adjust to taste
- Season

Mustard Dressing

Extra virgin olive oil
1 tbsp Dijon mustard
Salt
Pepper

Place the mustard in a large bowl. Pour in about twice as much (in volume) oil and whisk until incorporated. Taste. If required, add another tbsp of oil and whisk again. Keep going until you get the flavour you want. Season to taste.

Wash and dry your chosen salad and just prior to serving. Toss in the dressing and enjoy.

ACCIDENTAL PIZZA

200g Strong Bread Flour
50g semolina
1 pack dried yeast (fast acting, of course!)
A pinch of pinch salt
A tsp of sugar
200ml lukewarm water
About ½ tube tomato puree
7 cloves garlic, peeled and crushed
50ml olive oil (or more, to your taste)
10 or so tomatoes, halved
Chopped basil

Mix the flour, semolina, yeast, sugar and salt. Add water and mix with spoon. When consolidated, tip out onto a floured surface and knead for about 5 minutes if you have time – I don't care what anyone says, I've done it in 3 minutes due to excessive Friday exhaustion and it still turns out great pizza! – it should feel soft and springy. Add more flour if too sticky, more water (carefully!) if too hard or dry.

Cover with a towel and leave for 30 minutes to rise.

In the meantime, mix the tomato puree, garlic and olive oil – make it to the texture you like.

Roll out to size of pizza tray, keeping well dusted with flour (approximately 30cm in size) and put onto tray. Cut crust off, unless feeling piggy, in which case leave until you've put on the topping and then roll it up in a pretty, rustic fashion – this is good to dip in sea salt, though very bad for you.

Spread with tomato puree then arrange the tomatoes. Put it in the oven, at about 170* for 20 – 30 minutes (look at the pizza, does it look good to you?). Bring out, sprinkle with a little Maldon Salt if feeling decadent and then the basil. Serve.

I made it at half quantities tonight as we decided we needed more than the pesto I'd made (we like food!). It was lovely and not too much. But I think this will make it onto the regular pizza rota – fantastic that it is cheese free!

FISH CURRY WITH VEGETABLE SAUCE

There are a lot of ingredients in this but it is still fairly quick and easy to make and a good starter curry for the kids.

2 tins coconut milk
½ tube tomato puree
Water / stock (I use the bottled stuff, very easy to use when cooking anything!)
5 cardamom pods, emptied with husks discarded
2 star anise
5 cm ginger, peeled and grated finely
5 cloves ginger – chopped or minced, whatever is easiest!
2 tsp ground cumin (or more if you like it!)
2 tsp ground coriander (ditto)
¼ tsp fenugreek
¼ tsp turmeric
100g ground almonds (as you wish or don't – tastes lovely without)
2 cauliflowers
4 carrots
4 sticks celery
2 potatoes
1kg white fish (chicken, prawns etc – whatever you prefer and in whatever quantities!)

Gently fry the ginger, garlic and spices in oil (I use olive) for up to 5 minutes. Add the coconut milk, water, stick, tomato puree and almonds if using. Bring to boil and simmer for 10 – 15 minutes.
Add chopped vegetables and cook until soft. Blend the mixture.
Put back to pan, heat gently and add chopped fish until cooked.
This makes a lot of curry. I got eight mini-meals for the freezer, (each serving 2 small children,) and then there was enough sauce for 3 portions to be frozen for me and the hubby. I'm going to add some frozen prawns to ours when we have it.

By the way, the kids both loved it!

CHICKEN TONIGHT à la WORKING MUM!

My eldest decided, after months of loving mushrooms, that she hated them and was going through an odd, hater-of-all-things-veg phase. She loves Chicken Tonight sauces whenever this is made for her (not by me, but I'm not a snob, I've always liked them too!). So, voilà, my own version of 'chicken tonight', which both of my gals love and down in minutes.

2 Roasted chickens (I buy fresh, roast then shred)
3 packs mushrooms – whatever you like, I vary
chicken stock (I pour straight from the bottle to taste or just add a cube)
2 cloves garlic, chopped
3 carrots
3 celery sticks
1 bay leaf
Water & whole milk in a ratio of 1:3, enough to cover all veg

Chop the veg. Heat all ingredients except the chicken and mushrooms in a pan and bring to simmer – allow to cook for 10 minutes then add the mushrooms. Leave to cook for another 10 minutes. Remove the bay leaf then blend the sauce. Add chicken, heat if necessary* then serve.

This recipe may make 6 or 7 meals for 2 kids and 3 or so more for myself and husband#1.

*This, like many of my meals, take more than the hour cut off I say – that's because I make loads and freeze it, remember! Next time it's very quick to defrost and reheat.

BEANS AND SAUSAGES

This was inspired in some way by cassoulet, though I know it is very different. For an even healthier version, you could swap the sausages for chicken portions – it would still be packed full of flavour.

1 onion, chopped
2 cloves garlic, chopped
1 chilli, chopped – deseed if necessary, leave out for kids
1 Tin passata (or tomatoes)
1 carrot, chopped
1 stick celery, chopped
1 pack sausages
1 tin butter beans (or beans of your choice)
Sun-dried tomatoes

Sweat the onion, garlic, chilli, celery and carrot in olive oil until softened but not golden. Add the sausages and allow to brown a little, maybe for 5 to 10 minutes. Add the passata, butter beans and sun dried tomatoes if used and bring to boil.

Place in an oven proof dish (my frying pan is oven proof, so brilliant for this) and put in a pre-heated oven of 200' for 30 to 40 minutes. Stir once after 15 minutes, but allow the top to brown after that.

If doing for kids, I do the sauce (usually double the quantities but no chilli) and then blend. I cook them chipolatas and add after. This freezes nicely and I add a tin of borlotti beans when reheating. They love it. In this version, the sausage fat is also discarded, so healthier.

SPAGHETTI WITH SARDINES, TOMATOES & MUSSELS

Our lovely and generous neighbour, Jack turned up with some onions and tomatoes so I quickly had to change tea from soup to pasta.

1 tin sardines
5 medium tomatoes, ripe, chopped
1 clove garlic, chopped
1 large onion, sliced
1 tin mussels

Sweat the onion in olive oil with the garlic. When softened, add the tomatoes. After five minutes, add the sardines and mussels. In the meantime cook some pasta (I like long, messy types, but that's just me). When the pasta is cooked add some capers to the sauce. Mix together and enjoy! A little black pepper goes well.

SUMMER VEGETABLE PASTA

Lovely and simple, Summer, vegetable pasta – cooks in the time it takes to make the spaghetti. And it has to be spaghetti, surely?

1 clove garlic, chopped
1 onion, sliced
French beans, chopped into 2cm lengths
Broad beans, podded, of course!
Courgette, ribboned
Mushrooms, chopped
1 tbsp liquid chicken stick
1tbsp balsamic vinegar
Parmesan cheese to taste

Sauté some garlic and onion in olive oil and then add vegetables in order of the time it will take to cook. So I put in my homegrown French beans (chopped up as they were a little past it) and broad beans in fairly early with chopped mushrooms and added my homegrown, ribboned courgette right near the end when I also added a little chicken stock and balsamic vinegar and heated quickly to reduce.

I finished it with a grating of parmesan and a sprinkling of salt at the end. Healthy, quick and easy.

TOMATO SALAD WITH BASIL & BALSAMIC DRESSING

Tomatoes – sliced
Basic, chopped (I use scissors, sorry purists!)
Balsamic vinegar
Extra Virgin Olive Oil

Slice the tomatoes and put on a plate, mix about 2/3 oil to 1/3 vinegar (in fact, just do it to taste!) and then mix together. Drizzle onto tomatoes and then add basil on top. Serve with crusty bread or as an accompaniment to fish or meat. Up to you, really!

VEGETABLE CANNELLONI

I did this for the girls when the youngest was only just really eating and I blended the vegetables completely, then had to cook the 'mush' to reduce the liquid. They loved it (as did my teenage niece who would often be there at feeding time!), but this time I've mashed the veg with a potato masher when cooked and only diced some of the stuff, so we gave more texture.

1 head broccoli
1 cauliflower
5 carrots, sliced and chopped in half
1 leek, sliced
3 portabella mushrooms, chopped
2 cloves garlic, chopped
1 tub ricotta
2 – 3 tins chopped tomatoes
Mozzerella or parmesan to top off
20 Cannelloni tubes

Chop the cauliflower and the broccoli and cook (boil, steam etc) until just done and mash. Meanwhile, fry the garlic, carrot, leek and garlic in a little olive oil until just softened and add the mushroom. Continue until cooked. Add to the mashed cauliflower and broccoli then stir in the ricotta. At this point season as you like – if you are making for kids, resist!

Oil a large lasagne dish. Stuff the mixture into the cannelloni tubes (this is messy – if not too hot, the kids can help!) and place the tubes into the dish. When finished, if there is mixture left, just spread over the top. Cover with the tomatoes and then sprinkle with the cheese.

Put into a medium over (about 180-190') for about 40 minutes or until the cannelloni is cooked. Enjoy.

NB, as with many of my recipes this allowed me to freeze meals for later – I think I fed the girls two cannelloni tubes each, Husband#1 and I would have three, maybe four – but you know what you can eat!

CHICKEN NOODLE SOUP

Ingredients per person:

A clove of garlic
1 – 2 chicken thighs, chopped into bite size pieces
1 shallot or small onion – why buy a bag of shallots?!
1 stalk of lemon grass or a kaffir lime leaf – often found in the
freezer isle
a handful of mushrooms
groundnut oil (olive oil will do)
Chicken / vegetable stock
Star anise
Noodles
Coriander
Lime to squeeze over

Peel and crush the garlic and shallot or onion. Bash the lemon grass with a rolling pin to release the flavour or simply have the kaffir lime leaves (2 or 3) ready. Heat a wok to medium and add a tablespoon or so of oil – add the garlic, shallot and lemon grass/kaffir lime leaves and stir for a minute – if the garlic starts to colour, just remove from the heat for a moment to cool but keep stirring Add the chicken and then the mushrooms and stir fry for a few minutes. Next, add the stock and the star anise and cook for five or so minutes. Finally add the noodles and allow to cook according to instructions. Before serving, season to taste, squeeze with lime and sprinkle with coriander.

If you want:

- Add thinly sliced carrots or peppers to mushrooms when stir frying
- Add thinly shredded cooked meat or prawns
- Add some greens one or two minutes before serving, if you like!

Lizzie McCall

HUMOUS

This makes enough for 2 – 4 depending on what you serve with it and what you serve it for. For lunch, with a couple of crispbreads, it will be good for two. I much prefer doing my own as I like the texture. I find shop bought humous is a little too sweet and often very smooth.

1 tin chick peas
2 – 3 garlic cloves
Juice of 1 lemon
Olive oil
1 tablespoon tahini (optional – as it can be an allergen)

Put drained chick peas, finely chopped garlic, lemon juice and tahini into blender and start. Add the olive oil until the humous reaches a texture you like.

If you want:
- Try adding a few olives
- A little chopped coriander goes nicely
- A deseeded finely chopped chilli is nice, but less garlic is required as garlic makes it hot
- Add one or two deseeded tomatoes
- Add sun dried tomatoes
- Slow roasted tomatoes are good to add
- Mixed roasted vegetables add a lovely flavour: courgettes, red onions, peppers and tomatoes

LIZZIE'S FISH PIE

Enough for 4, but don't take much notice of my measurements, for example with the potatoes, as I always make loads. Put in whatever fish and/or shellfish you like to be honest, prawns and mussels are lovely:

1 Kg potatoes
Butter for mash
Whole milk to poach fish
1 smoked haddock fillet – go natural, who needs yellow fish?
1 piece salmon or cod or unsmoked haddock
Prawns – chop them up to make more plentiful!
Frozen Peas
Cheddar Cheese
Cornflour
1 egg, whisked
Salt & pepper
Parsley if you want, nice without in my opinion

- Set oven to gas mark 6
- Peel, chop and boil potatoes then mash with a little butter and then whisk in the egg. Set aside until needed.
- Put enough milk and a little water into a pan, so that it covers the fish and bring to the boil. Simmer for 8 minutes, making sure milk doesn't boil over (the water should help stop this)
- Remove fish and put on a plate. Keep milk.
- Flake the fish – not too small – checking for bones, but there shouldn't be many
- Thicken milk with cornflour and a little butter and season to taste.
- Mix flaked fish, prawns, peas and parsley. Put into a fairly deep casserole dish, then ladle over sauce one at a time and mix gently. You don't want too much sauce, you can always serve it as a gravy after cooking.
- Spoon mash over the top and gently smooth at the edges – you need enough potato to cover the whole pie and then grate Cheddar over the top.

- Bake for 30 minutes and serve with broccoli or vegetable of your choice.

If you like:

- When sauce has been thickened, add the zest and juice of a lemon
- Add a few flakes of saffron to the milk when cooking the fish, but don't use smoked fish, just use normal haddock in this case.
- Use smoked salmon – just chop into the mixture when it is put into the dish.
- Put some cheddar into the sauce when it is being thickened.
- Add mushrooms, cooked before adding to mixture
- Use chicken instead of fish, but steam it over water rather than poaching in milk. The sauce can be made by cooking some chopped mushrooms in a little milk & water, thickening it, seasoning it as before.

MINESTRONE

I love to make the minestrone and always pre-roast a joint of ham beforehand. Please don't sniff at the authenticity of the recipe, where I live you have to adapt and 'knuckle ends' of palma ham or pancetta are not hard to get, but impossible and supermarkets have refused to sell me them unsliced. I wonder if there is a possible weapon to be made from it?

☐ A small smoked ham joint
1 onion
3 stalks of celery
A fennel bulb
2 bay leaves
Finely chopped basil, including stalks
3 cloves of garlic, minced
2 glasses of red wine (if you wouldn't drink it, don't cook with it!)
1500ml chicken stock
2 tbsp tomato puree
Pack of French beans, halved
Two tins of tomatoes
Two tins of borlotti beans
A pack of spinach
Spaghetti – as much as you want, but maybe 20g per person if having bread as well
Parmesan to grate on top

Sautée the onion, celery, carrots and fennel with a bay leaf, some finely chopped basil stalks with leaves and three chopped garlic cloves in olive oil until softened. Then, add (a couple of glasses of) red wine, two tins of tomatoes and about a litre and a half of chicken stock, not to forget a couple of tablespoons of tomato puree. Put in some French beans and leave it to cook for ten or so minutes before adding broken up spaghetti or other pasta type – whatever you prefer. Near the end, put in two tins of borlotti beans, the chopped, smoked ham, and the spinach,
Serve with grated parmesan on top and crusty bread if you haven't overdone the pasta as I would!

Oh, and choose the pasta type you most like, not what a book tells you!

Finally, use the veg you want to use. Life is too short to use spring greens because they are in season, if you can't stand them.

CHICKEN AND SWEETCORN SOUP

This was a totally accidental discovery, we had some sweetcorn and hadn't used it – what to do? I remember a lobster and sweetcorn chowder I'd seen made where the whole cob is used to give extra flavour and I thought why not try a simpler but equally delicious dish?

2 packs (500g) of skinned and boned chicken thighs, chopped into smaller pieces
4 corn on the cobs
1 onion, chopped
1 clove of garlic, crushed or chopped finely
Olive oil
Chicken Stock
Corn flour for thickening
Salt and pepper as required

Sauté the garlic and union until soft but not browned then add the chicken and allow to cook. Meanwhile using a sharp knife, cut the corn from the cobs – to it over a bowl to catch the ones that try to get away! Once the chicken has coloured on all sides, add the sweetcorn as well as at least two of the cobs (depends on how large your pan its!) and enough stock to cover all of the ingredients. Cook for about 10 minutes. At this point mix about 1 tablespoon of cornflour with cold water and add to the soup, stirring all the time until it is a thickness that you like. Add more or less, depending on how you like it! Remove the cobs and serve.

This makes about 8 portions and freezes nicely for a later date.

SUMMER VEGETABLE SALAD WITH FETA

This was one of those lovely meals which ends up in your lunchbox or on your plate purely by accident. We'd grown French beans – both green and yellow this year and they'd grown well. The problem was they all got to a decent size at a point when I had few options to add them to a meal. So I picked them and blanched them and thought I could freeze for a later date when I'd stir fry in olive oil and crushed garlic – lovely. But then I thought about a salad and then noticed a lot of our tomatoes were also ripening together…hey presto, a salad was born! We had this for a starter on a Saturday night, but the next time it went into a lunchbox, but without the Feta.

French beans
Tomatoes – varied if possible!
Black olives
Feta (you could also use a lower fat variety, I did)
Balsamic vinegar
Extra virgin olive oil

Blanch and then cool the beans, chop the tomatoes and mix all together in a bowl. Add the olives and Feta, cubed. Then mix together extra virgin olive oil and balsamic vinegar (to taste, but probably use 2/3 oil and 1/3 vinegar) then pour over the salad.

ABOUT THE AUTHOR

Lizzie McCall is a working mum with two growing children. She lives in England with her husband, children and small array of household pets. Lizzie and her husband grow tomatoes, courgettes and beans in the summer and would love the time and space to do more!

Proof

Made in the USA
Charleston, SC
13 August 2015